mankiller poems

©2022 Wilma Mankiller

ISBN 979-8-9852632-4-4

Published by Pulley Press, an imprint of
Clyde Hill Publishing

Cover and book design by Dan D Shafer
Front cover photograph courtesy Cherokee Nation
Back cover photograph by Charlie Soap

Proceeds from this book will benefit the
Wilma Mankiller Foundation

mankiller poems

the lost poetry of

the Principal Chief of the Cherokee Nation **wilma mankiller**

FOREWORD BY

JOY HARJO

COMMENTARY BY

MARK TRAHANT

PULLEY PRESS

CONTENTS

FOREWORD

These poems are from one of the "Real People," Cherokee
Chief and change maker, Wilma Mankiller. Making poetry
is demanding as the wind as it carves sky. Breath, when
shaped by poetry, gives the soul a place to speak and sing.
With the publication of Mankiller's poems we are reminded
of her presence when she walked among us. Her words are
tracks made into songs on paper that still speak through the
years of a life, a time, a generation.

Joy Harjo
2022

NOTES FROM THE EDITORS

Three years before she became Principal Chief of the Cherokee Nation in 1985, Wilma Mankiller published six poems in a student magazine at Bacone College in Muskogee, Oklahoma. Her biography, which she wrote, appeared in the magazine as:

> *Wilma Mankiller, from Stilwell, Oklahoma, is Cherokee. She is 36 years of age, the mother of two teenage girls and works as a grants writer and community organizer for the Cherokee Nation of Oklahoma in Tahlequah.*

> *Wilma, as one of eleven children, began writing at about age ten as a method of expressing her individuality in a large, lively, creative family. She has always used writing to express feelings and emotions that she found difficult to express verbally.*

> *Besides poetry, she writes essays and has an interest in writing short stories.*

When she was eleven years old, Wilma Mankiller and her family moved to San Francisco as part of a federal "relocation" program from Oklahoma. This was an ill-conceived federal effort to move Native Americans into cities where there were supposed to be more jobs. In fact, the program resembled various attempts at "assimilation," the idea that Native American culture, language, and people would disappear. She lived in the Bay Area until she was thirty—there, she wrote poems as a young activist with the Occupation of Alcatraz and the Pit River Tribe, while a college student and mother. She continued writing poems when she moved back to Oklahoma in 1976, worked for the Cherokee Nation, fell in love with Cherokee traditionalist and community helper Charlie Soap, and served as Principal Chief and beyond, until her death in 2010.

The poems are presented here in an order that we hope indicates Wilma's personal and professional journey: from Native woman finding her identity, to the challenges of a forced move into a city, into a journey home where she finds love and leadership.

With the help of Charlie Soap, Wilma's husband, we gathered these poems from her barn at Mankiller Flats in Adair County, Oklahoma in the pandemic summer of 2021, during August days of more than one-hundred degree heat. In a metal building full of cardboard and plastic boxes, we thumbed through mold-pocked documents, old books, trophies, contents of desk drawers, recipes, and medical research— hoping to come across poems. Midday, we took breaks and had lunch with Charlie on the old basketball court where the rim was bent down over us. Then, we'd resume our work in the barn. At first, we found a few poems and then, as the days went on, we found more. Running these poems from the barn into print, as if glided along on a pulley system from Mankiller Flats to a bigger audience, shows how an activist reflected on her life through art, and that art itself is activism.

Frances McCue and Greg Shaw, Pulley Press

CONTEXT IS EVERYTHING

Mark Trahant

In 2009, a year before she died, Wilma sent me an email with the subject line, "Context is Everything." She was asking me to edit a paper she'd written about philanthropy and the lack of investment in Native communities. I thought of that subject line as I read these poems. In fact, this collection provides the context that's been missing from discussions of Wilma.

So many of us know Wilma Mankiller as a tribal leader, as a philanthropist, and as an American icon. These poems give us more because they transport us to another time when Wilma had yet to figure it all out.

I discovered three ways to read her poems. On their own: Wilma invites us to play with language, love, culture, identity, and the human spirit. Or, as a way to learn more about Wilma's inner reflections: she tells us how to be the "Real People" and to accept the friendship of the wind. And third, we can read these poems already knowing a bit about her journey and discover a few of the physical and emotional milepost markers that take us from Alcatraz to Pit River to

Wounded Knee. Throughout, her journey is punctuated by geography, places that she loved. They are far more than dots on a map.

"I care about Cuba, South Africa, Jemez Pueblo, Navajo, Bosnia and Jay, Oklahoma," she writes. "Some would say not womanly things to care about..." Line by line, Wilma discovers herself, and yet we are the ones who learn more of the context of such a public life.

SMOKE SIGNALS

Nowadays tribal people make fun
of smoke signals
but there was a time when messages
had to be sent long distances
from one camp to another

The wind carries these messages
which sometimes called for a great meeting
to discuss important news or to gather people
for a spiritual event

Even today the smoke from ceremonial fires
carries messages along the wind
sometimes even to the heavens
but no one can read them anymore

But that doesn't mean the
messages aren't there

12 **REAL PEOPLE**

In the time of the ancients
      we called ourselves
      Real People

After countless seasons of "civilization"
      we remain
      Real People

We gather to speak about
      kinship
      our relationship to the stars
      the sacred fire

While the blue-veined talk on cell phones about
      mutual funds
      the right schools
      and always and forever
      their looks and weight

Do they possess the ability to love
      or just play a role in
      dreary
      predictable lives

Have they forgotten (if they ever knew)
      how to
      accept the friendship of the wind
      or love deeply and radically

Maybe they really are another species
      not
      Real People

14

CAN ANYONE ELSE HEAR?

grandma Gourd listens to the
                longing cries of November
as December spreads crystal flakes
                over the tired body of our
                sweet Mother in slumber

she strains her ears to hear the
                wolves of silver howling
                in anticipation of the winter's chill
and the faint sound of the wings
                of a raven beating in the falling snow

as the moist beads of a cold snow
                begin to form a circle of lonely
                thoughts that make her wonder
if there are others who can still hear

she remembers
                that the sound of a million
                colored televisions
                has drowned out almost all
                echoes of our being

SUNLIGHT AND DREAMS

The unreasonably warm day marked the end
of a bitter, icy winter
as Sun graciously warmed the Earth
tender young plants stretched and pushed their way up through the soil
to gratefully lean into her nourishing light

A tiny wisp of wind whispered through the infant plants
urging them to dance in the late
morning sun

The People were in ceremony to acknowledge
changing seasons
offer thanksgiving prayers for life
and the generous gifts of the Earth

As the sweet laughter of children rang
out in the heart of the village circle
everything seems perfectly in balance
then suddenly things shifted and changed
the sky filled with angry dark clouds
hiding the sun and blocking out the light

The violent sounds of the Thunder Beings shocked
everyone into silence

A hard, ill wind darkly spun its way
through the treetops
down to the Earth

CONTINUES...

It was a northerly wind
North
The land of blue-veined people
North
The land of death
North
The color of blue

The North wind caused the sun to hide
while it swept away the People's dreams

20 **REALITY**

the sane reality of daily routine
leaves me stale...
daydreams elude me
so I talk to a crow
who looks like he may
know the secret of the Redbirds

FINDING REDBIRD

Mark Trahant

Wilma Mankiller wanted to talk about her ideas, and how to make them happen. She kept her focus and, day by day, stripped away false notions about gender and leadership. She found a way to engage people in a conversation about the future and, in 1985, two years after she won her first election as Deputy Chief, she moved into the office of Principal Chief of the Cherokee Nation (her mentor, Ross Swimmer, had been appointed to a new job in the Reagan administration).

Mankiller's ideas were always her strength. She said it was so important to have a national conversation about race that included peeling away false stereotypes and adding tribal accounts and philosophies to a shared narrative. That included stories. And images. And names.

Once, I remember that a young man asked Wilma Mankiller what he should call her. She was then Principal Chief of the Cherokee Nation and twice-elected as the leader of some 200,000 people. But this young man was uncomfortable with what he figured was a "male" term.

"Should we address you as 'Chieftain-ess'?" he asked.

Mankiller didn't say a word. Then, after hearing the suggestion "Chiefette," she finally responded. She told the man to call her "Ms. Chief" or "MissChief."

Wilma Mankiller made so much mischief. Just as the crow in her poem "Reality" who may "know the secret of the Redbirds," Wilma had her own history that gave her insight into her own life, and those of the tribe, and she transformed that into poems. The poems that follow trace some of the hard times she faced in San Francisco and her journey back to live on her grandfather's allotment in Adair County, Oklahoma.

Wilma was still looking for the secrets of Redbird. I recalled a time when she told me about Redbird, as in Redbird Smith. He was a Cherokee leader who resisted US policy in the late 19th century, especially the Dawes Commission. Redbird Smith had this ideal for a Cherokee community, a notion that must have appealed to Wilma. But a secret? The quote she told me: "Our forces have been dissipated by external forces; perhaps it has been just a training, but we must now get together as a race and render our contributions to mankind."

"I know what happened to our people," Mankiller said. And until that same story is taught—or at least respected—by the rest of the nation, there cannot be an honest dialogue.

And Mankiller successfully changed the nature of the national story because, as she once said, "I can eliminate any stereotypes about what a chief looks like." Of course, the Redbirds could have just been the wind. The wind will always have stories to tell.

OKTAHA

he's been on the road for more than
        a lifetime
        and still the hunt goes on
from Alcatraz to Pit River to Wounded Knee
        from the rich red clay of his homeland
        to the streets of San Francisco
        hunger for the food of his soul
        urges him on
maybe someday when he stops to rest in
        the shadows of a cave,
        drinks in the cool, clear streams
        of an ancient spring
his thoughts will take him back
        to a time when the wind was a child
and he will know that if he looks
        into the eyes of a blue panther
        he can find the tempo of his vision

MOVING ON

cold, hard times have left me
     wounded and scarred but...
i can still feel the warm lips of life
     kissing my heart; stirring my mind
urging me to go on until i can
     find the lies of my own making and
     battle them in moonlit meadows

30 **THE MOON**

maybe I should not talk of the Moon
     but lay back down and just believe

that once the Moon held my fragile mind
     in his gleaming hands

while I smiled and let him paw at my soul

WORKING LADIES

I can sometimes hear the longing
        cries of my sister the prostitute
as she moves in a daze from one
        pointless encounter
        to another

sometimes in the shadow of the
        soft, sweet smile of the moon
        she tries to believe that there is
        a flicker of love
        in a hurried embrace

And as I
        move along the blue carpets
        of the Cherokee Nation
        trying to believe there is a
        flicker of hope

I feel solidarity with my sister

LEAVING SAN FRANCISCO

at night she is like an aging beauty queen—
 she sparkles
 looks quiet
 elegant
even her brightest lights do not look tawdry,
but in the bright sunny morning,
 she shows it all
at night you cannot see
 the lost children
 skinny junkies looking for a fix
 wasted young warriors searching for
 an alternative that doesn't exist
 hopeless elders in lobbies of ancient,
 damp hotels
but in the morning, she shows it all
 she looks so old,
 corrupt,
 used,
 hard
stripped of the magic of night, it's easy
to see she has been through her prime
and is on the way down
i am not going with her

36 **THE BLUES**

got the Stormy Monday Blues on
    Thursday night
    lost
    without form
hoping fantasies will rise
like the sweet smell of cedar
to touch the sleepless mind

WHERE ARE YOUR WOMEN?

Mark Trahant

While Wilma Mankiller was the first woman to lead the Cherokee
Nation, the nation's second-largest tribe, she was a prominent
national citizen, too, a regular voice for Native people and women's
issues. Mankiller started working at the Cherokee Nation in 1977 in
the community development department, focusing on the plights of
children and families. She then ran for the office of Deputy Chief
in 1983.

That election was rough because so many voters only wanted to talk
about why a woman was running. It had never happened before.

Wilma once gave a speech at Emory University where she told a story
about when the United States first sent a treaty negotiation team to
meet with the Cherokees. One of the first questions the tribe asked
was: "Where are your women?" Unlike the group of men sent by the
Federal Government, Cherokee women were present at important
ceremonies and negotiations—and it was inconceivable that the
representatives from the Federal Government would come alone.

How could you negotiate anything with only half of your people or half of a way of thinking? The logic is flawed: How can any society negotiate (or govern) with only half its people, half its logic, half of its humanity?

Half of humanity was missing from our leadership, and Wilma knew it: "And as I move along the blue carpets of the Cherokee Nation," Wilma wrote, "(I am) trying to believe there is a flicker of hope."

In her poem "Working Ladies," she writes: "I feel solidarity with my sister." In her life, she was finding partnership with Charlie Soap, a man who supported her work fully and deeply.

Wilma's solidarity is a flicker, stronger now, as the list of Native women in leadership grows, and must grow more: chief, chair, governor, senator, member of Congress, trustee, director, leader, president, and philanthropist. So many firsts in our continuing evolution as Real People. And so many yet to be.

"Where are your women?" Wilma might ask and then answer, "Here."

I WANT TO BE REINCARNATED
AS GLORIA STEINEM

If I am ever reincarnated
I want to come back as
        Gloria Steinem

so I can have a sharp mind
        a quick wit
and a faith in people
that never wavers or doubts

so I can be a sister to
all things in the creation
women, men, children
plants, animals, the stars,
        water and the wind

so I can face all life's
burdens squarely and
dance anyway

so I can work tirelessly for a just
society and find something
        to laugh about every day

so I can be one of the most
important women of the century
and remain genuinely humble and
despite everything
still express love unconditionally

CONTINUES...

I want to be reincarnated as
Gloria Steinem

so I can live
a full, joyful life with few regrets
except perhaps not going to the
       beach a little more

THIS THING CALLED LOVE

Trying to say words about love is
　　　　like trying to reach out
　　　　and hold the wind
I can feel it,
　　　　I know it is there
　　　　but it can't be captured
sometimes I try to express love by sharing
　　　　secrets in awkward moments and
　　　　strange laughter
but I always feel
　　　　so much more
　　　　than I can ever express
better I should try to hold the wind
　　　　than try to say words about
　　　　this thing called love

48 **A NIGHT ALONE**

his warmth seems so far away/
the fingers that strum the
chords of mystery are still/
the moon is dim/tonight is cold/
and hot tea just doesn't taste
quite as good as the fruits of love

50

BEGINNINGS OF A SONG *for Charlie*

Standing on the edge of twilight,
        looking for a sign

Father Thunder comes to talk about
        the Fall of Mankind

Lady River weaves her way
        past his everyday life

Tells a tale of the night
        she became
        a winter storm's wife

His mind starts to show
        what he could be

If his human eyes
        could see

Standing on the edge of twilight
        looking for a sign

That the old medicine is not lost
        to all mankind

52 **WAITING FOR MAY**

Cool spring days keep me huddled
 by a warm stove and I
 long to let
 my feet touch the dirt
 of the Earth's calm ways
so I can be reminded again of
 just why we are here

COMFORT

locked in the safety of comfort
     unmoved by the sounds of life
the thoughts of my untamed soul
     used to drift so I could hear
     the sunshine speak as Lady Dawn
     gave way to the sweet melodies
     of a morning song
and I did, once, long ago
     drink the ancient nectar
     of an autumn moon
used to live down by the river,
     lie on the rich red clay banks
     watching the sleepy sun dance
and just listen to the loud whispers
     of moods that could still move me
but now, it's just cups of coffee,
     wicked dreams and an occasional glance
     at what used to be
I'm still locked in the safety of comfort
     unmoved by the sounds of life

56 **REALITY {AGAIN}**

When the land darkens, I close my eyes
and dream of a world of my own making
Visions of druids, stars, the fire,
trees that whisper ancient secrets

I dream into existence a universe
without hatred,
where no one betrays me

In sun's warm light, I care about Cuba,
South Africa, Jemez Pueblo, Navajo,
Bosnia and Jay, Oklahoma
Some would say
not womanly things to care about

In sleep I refresh myself and dream
of a time when thunder spoke to me
the moon smiled on me and
told me I was one of them

Or maybe I will just listen to
the messages from long ago
sent along pathways of the wind

The wind will have stories to tell
and when I wake up
I won't really know whether I dreamed the stories
or they are real
but then
I never could tell the difference anyway

58 **FEELING**

i kiss the rare fruits of joy
     and feel the heat of being alive
embracing closely the lights of
     fading dreams
as they circle the edges of
     something called freedom

ACKNOWLEDGMENTS

"Reality," "A Night Alone," "Leaving San Francisco," "Can Anyone Else Hear Me?," "The Moon," "The Blues," "Oktaha," "Comfort," "Feelings," and "Moving On" were originally published in *Echoes of Our Being* by the Tahlequah Indian Writers Group, Indian University Press, Bacone College, 1982, edited by Robert J. Conley.

Several of the poems were dated: "Real People" (October 1999); "Beginnings of a Song" (1979, 1983, and 2007); "Reality" (1998).

"I Want to Be Reincarnated as Gloria Steinem" was in the collection of Kristina Kiehl and ended with "Happy Birthday, Love Wilma."

The remaining poems were retrieved from Mankiller's barn by Greg Shaw and Frances McCue, with permission by Charlie Soap.

CONTRIBUTORS

JOY HARJO is an internationally renowned performer and writer of the Muscogee (Creek) Nation. She is serving her second term as the 23rd Poet Laureate of the United States.

The author of nine books of poetry, including the highly acclaimed *An American Sunrise*, several plays, and children's books, and two memoirs, *Crazy Brave* and *Poet Warrior*, her many honors include the Ruth Lily Prize for Lifetime Achievement from the Poetry Foundation, the Academy of American Poets Wallace Stevens Award, two NEA fellowships, and a Guggenheim Fellowship. As a musician and performer, Harjo has produced seven award-winning music albums including her newest, *I Pray for My Enemies*. She is Executive Editor of the anthology *When the Light of the World was Subdued, Our Songs Came Through—A Norton Anthology of Native Nations Poetry*, and the editor of *Living Nations, Living Words: An Anthology of First Peoples Poetry*, the companion anthology to her signature Poet Laureate project. She is a chancellor of the Academy of American Poets, Board of Directors Chair of the Native Arts & Cultures Foundation, and is the first Artist-in-Residence for Tulsa's Bob Dylan Center. She lives in Tulsa, Oklahoma.

MARK TRAHANT is a citizen of the Shoshone–Bannock Tribes and editor-at-large for *Indian Country Today*. In 2017 Trahant was hired to return the "newspaper" to life after it had gone out of business. Trahant moved the nonprofit company from its Washington, DC base to Phoenix, Arizona in 2019. It is now located at the Walter Cronkite School of Journalism and Mass Communication at Arizona State University. In March 2021, *ICT* became an independent news company, owned by its nonprofit arm, IndiJ Public Media. Trahant shifted roles in January 2022 and is now leading the Indigenous Economics Project for *ICT*.

Trahant has been a professor at the University of North Dakota, the University of Alaska Anchorage, the University of Idaho, and the University of Colorado. He is a member of the American Academy of Arts and Sciences.

CPSIA information can be obtained
at www.ICGtesting.com
Printed in the USA
BVHW041214090622
639342BV00002B/255